The Bites of Mexico

80 Recipes of Authentic Mexican Snacks, Appetizers, Sauces, Dips, Drinks, Seasonings, Salsa, and Much More!

MARISSA MARIE

D1113245

TABLE OF CONTENTS

MEXICAN COOKING FUNDAMENTALS

Cooking Mexican food in an authentic way can seem like a daunting task, but like everything else in life, some guidance and a bit of practice is all you need. I'll take care of the guidance part, and I will leave it to you to take care of the rest!

Mexican food has an insane variety, and the taste easily covers a wide spectrum of flavours. Most American cooks can cook great Mexican food, but are sometimes a little off the mark from authentic Mexican flavour. The primary objective of this book is to enable an average non-Mexican cook to cook authentic Mexican food using the tools and ingredients easily available in any corner of the world.

In this section, we will look at some of the ingredients, equipment, and techniques you will need to know about before you can achieve great results with Mexican cooking. Keep at it, and you'll be preparing full-course Mexican dinners in no time!

THE FLAVOURS OF MEXICO

All regional cuisine has its distinct flavour, and Mexican food is no exception. You can tell when Mexican food is cooking nearby just by the smell. Mexican food gets its distinct flavour from the combination of ingredients that are commonly used in Mexican food. A few of these ingredients are: cilantro, cumin, chiles, garlic, etc. Once you get a hang of the Mexican flavour and ingredient combinations, you will be able to give a Mexican twist to pretty much every recipe in the world!

Latin markets are great places to stock up on supplies for cooking Mexican food. If you're in the USA or UK, you probably have such a market in close vicinity. You can easily find nearby markets using Google. If there is an ingredient, you're having problem finding, amazon.com is always a great last resort.

I will try my best to keep things simple, and will only use ingredients that are easy to source.

MEXICAN STAPLES

In order to achieve close to authentic Mexican flavour, you will need to have full understanding of the ingredients that make food taste Mexican. In this section we will talk about a few of the Mexican staples that you will absolutely need to include in your kitchen pantry, if you're serious about Mexican cooking.

Feel free to buy canned/preserved versions of the ingredients if you can't find fresh ones.

CHILE

Chile is an indispensable ingredient for Mexican cooking, and we use a wide variety of these here in Mexico. The recipes in this book call for wide variety of these, so make sure you know where to source them. A nearby Latin market or store is a great place to

look, or you can always find these online on www.amazon.com ,
or www.mexgrocer.com .

ANCHO

This dried poblano sports a deep, smoky flavour that couples
great with beef and appears in an quite a few Mexican soups and
salsas. It needs to be reconstituted.

ARBOL

Less hot, but just as flavourful as the habanero, this brittle, dried
chile doesn't need reconstituting when added to soups, pots of
pinto beans, or tequila.

GUAJILLO

Fragrant, earthy, and rather spicy, this dried chile is essential to
moles and is commonly used as a purée in red chile sauces.

HABANERO

Deliciously fruity and super spicy (up to 350,000 Scoville units),
this usually orange, lantern-like pepper is an essential ingredient
of bottled hot sauces, tongue-singeing sauces, soups, and salsas.

JALAPEÑO

This most common of chile peppers is picked while green and
usually used fresh in pretty much everything Mexican.

MORITA (DRIED CHIPOTLE)

This slightly fruity, dried chile is a smoke-dried jalapeño. When dried, it needs reconstituting. When canned and sold as chipotle en adobo, both the chile itself and its amazingly useful sauce can lend smoky depth to the recipes it is used in.

POBLANO

This mild, dark-skinned chile pepper turns into ancho when dried. When fresh, it can be roasted or turned into a vessel for Chiles Rellenos.

SERRANO

Smaller and hotter than a jalapeño, this important fresh pepper is commonly included raw into relishes and salsas. It is sometimes used roasted.

HERBS AND SPICES

ACHIOTE PASTE

Made using super-hard annatto seeds, this paste adds a smoky, peppery flavour to marinades and sauces. It's usually diluted using sour orange and serves as an important ingredient in quite a few Mexican recipes.

ALLSPICE

These peppercorn-looking berries are usually toasted and ground to impart warmth to salsas, moles, and stews. To save time, buy it ground.

BAY LEAVES

Thinner than other varieties, Mexican bay laurel adds its amazing flavour to marinades, soups, and stews.

CILANTRO

This self-seeding annual is used fresh across Mexican salsas, rice dishes, soups, and moles. It's also commonly used to garnish tacos.

CINNAMON

Mexican cinnamon, or Ceylon cinnamon, is quite unlike the cinnamon normally used in the United States—it's headier and warmer than its American counterpart. It can be found in Mexican markets as sticks or ground. If you can't find Mexican cinnamon, use whichever version you have on hand.

CUMIN

Strong, earthy cumin seeds, for which there is no equivalent, are commonly toasted and ground and used in stews and soups.

MARJORAM

Usually used with thyme and oregano to flavour stews, this fragrant herb also appears as a component of pickled vegetables.

OREGANO

Different from the Mediterranean variety, the Mexican herb is often used dry in pozole and tomato-based soups, or in main dishes.

SESAME (AJONJOLÍ)

An important ingredient in moles, these nutty seeds are also used in baked goods, including on sandwich rolls.

THYME

This aromatic perennial is often used to pickle vegetables and to dry and use in combination with oregano and marjoram for flavouring stews and other slow-simmered dishes.

OTHER INGREDIENTS

AVOCADOS

This mild fruit finds is a common ingredient in many Mexican recipes. Simply halve, pit, and peel.

CAJETA

Similar to dulce de leche, this caramel sauce is a common ingredient in multiple desserts and is used to top ice cream. Look for Coronado brand, which is made from goat's milk and has a full, rich flavour. Cow's milk versions can also be used.

CHEESE

Cheese is a staple in the Mexican kitchen. A few of the popular kinds of cheese in Mexico are: cotija, queso Oaxaca, queso fresco, and Chihuahua.

CHOCOLATE

Mexican chocolate is indispensable for moles. Unsweetened cocoa is great as a background note for sauces and stews, because it lends wonderful depth.

CORN

Sweet corn is indispensable for on-the-cob elotes, as well as in salads and soups.

GARLIC

Whether roasted or used raw in salsas, these cloves are a vital ingredient in Mexican Cooking.

HOT SAUCE

Popular hot sauces among Mexican cooking newbies are: mild Tapatío or Valentina; Cholula; and El Yucateco's Salsa Picante de Habanero.

LIMES

Keep plenty of limes on hand—they're indispensable for adding a spritz of citrusy brightness to finished dishes, as well as to salsas and cocktails.

ONIONS

Red and white/yellow onions are vital ingredients in Mexican cooking. Red ones are used for pickling and using fresh, while white/yellow ones are used in blended salsas as well as soups, stews, and pretty much everything else savory.

TORTILLAS

You can buy these or make your own. I will show you how in the next section.

VINEGAR

White, apple cider, and sometimes sugarcane vinegar add acidic pungency to pickled vegetables, vinaigrettes, and one-pot meals. Fruit vinegars are called for in quite a few Mexican recipes too.

EQUIPMENT

Improvisation is a talent every good cook has. Don't have an ingredient or appliance that a recipe calls for? Just improvise! However, too much improvisation can take a toll on the final result, which is why I will recommend having at least a few basic things in your kitchen if you are serious about Mexican cooking.

THE ESSENTIALS

COMAL

Any old cast iron or non-stick griddle will do the job. If you don't have any of these, you can get a comal, which is the traditional Mexican griddle used to make tortillas, sopes, quesadillas, etc. It is also a handy tool for dry roasting.

DUTCH OVEN

This little appliance is great for slow-cooking, and if you don't have one yet, you would do well to invest in one. If you don't know where to look, just pick up one from amazon.

MOLCAJETE

Mexican recipes sometimes require you to crush stuff. Might as well do it using a traditional Mexican tool. If you don't wish to invest in one, any old crushing tool will do the job.

STEAMER

Quite a few Mexican staples such as *tamales* require steaming. There are many ways of steaming if you don't have a steamer and don't wish to invest in one, just google them.

TORTILLA PRESS

If you ever get tired of rolling out tortillas and other stuff using a rolling pin, just remember that you can always make your work much easier by investing in a tortilla press. These are cheap, and easily available online, and in stores.

THE TIME-SAVERS

All the appliances in this section exist purely to save time. If you have a lot of free time on your hands, feel free to skip to the next section.

BLENDER OR IMMERSION BLENDER

Mexican sauces, drinks, salsas, etc. call for quite aa lot of puréeing and pulsing. Having an electric appliance that does the job at the press of a button sure helps.

FOOD PROCESSOR

Mexican food has a LOT of chopped up stuff. If you don't wish to do the chopping manually, invest in an electric food processor.

PRESSURE COOKER

Pressure cooking is the most efficient cooking method known to man. It is quick, cheap, and doesn't allow for much wastage of energy. It would be a good idea to invest in an electric or traditional pressure cooker if you don't have one already.

SLOW COOKER

Slow cooking really allows the flavours to be incorporated into the dishes, and is a great tool to have in your kitchen.

BASIC TECHNIQUES

If you've been cooking for a while, you will know all the basic techniques mentioned in this section. If you're a newbie, read through this section, and also watch a few videos on YouTube if you don't understand the procedure.

BLISTERING

To blacken and blister chiles, roast them directly over a gas flame for approximately five minutes, turning using tongs until charred and blistered. Another method is to broil them 4 inches beneath a preheated broiler for approximately ten minutes. Then, place them in a bowl, and cover the bowl using a kitchen towel to steam. After about five minutes, remove and discard the stem and seeds, and peel away and discard the blackened skin.

BRAISING

Using an enameled cast iron Dutch oven, which retains and uniformly distributes heat, sear seasoned meat on all sides in shimmering-hot oil on moderate to high heat to accomplish deep caramelization. If sautéing vegetables, remove and reserve browned meat before this step (and return it to the pot once done). Deglaze the pot by pouring in the braising liquid, using a wooden spoon to scrape the browned, tasty bits from the bottom of the pan, as they will enhance the flavour of the dish. Place the meat back into the pot, along with any juices that accumulated while it was resting. Bring the liquid to a simmer, cover the pot, and move it to a preheated 325°F oven to finish cooking until it becomes fall-apart tender.

DRY ROASTING

Dry roasting means applying heat to "dry" foods, such as unpeeled garlic, tomatoes, tomatillos, onions, or chiles. It can be done using a skillet, cast iron skillet, or comal.

GRILLING

Grilling is called for in quite a few Mexican recipes. The process is simple, as long as you have a grill. Keep it clean, well oiled, and preheat it before you throw the food on it.

GRINDING

You can do this in three ways. The most popular method is to pulverize them using a mortar and pestle, or molcajete, a kitchen tool you can also use to bruise herbs and mash ingredients for guacamole. The second way is to use a spice grinder, perfect for larger jobs. Finally, a third option is a Microplane, great for grating nutmeg, cinnamon, chocolate, citrus zest, and garlic.

RECONSTITUTING

Dried chiles have an incredible depth of flavour, and they're something you'll use a lot when cooking Mexican recipes. While ground, dried chiles may sometimes be used as a substitute, just follow this procedure. For up to eight peppers, fill a small saucepan with water and bring to the boiling point over high heat. Take the pan off the heat, and immerse the peppers in the hot water. Let them reconstitute for about half an hour. Drain, discard the water, and use in recipes as required.

STEAMING

My favourite steaming method is using a covered Dutch oven or pot with a tight-fitting rack placed inside. To steam tamales, use a large covered pot outfitted with either a rack or a perforated steamer basket that sits above the water line. Bring the water to the boiling point, place the tamales in the basket, cover, and steam until the masa dough becomes firm and easily pulls away from the corn husk. The process takes approximately ninety minutes.

TOASTING SPICES

This technique enhances the flavour of spices, while mellowing them out at the same time. In a skillet over moderate heat, toast spices just until aromatic, shaking the pan once in a while to avoid burning. Then, move them to a mortar, or molcajete, for grinding.

SALSA, SAUCES, & SEASONINGS

Fresh homemade salsa is the best salsa. Restaurants may or may not use fresh ingredients, and store-bought ready to eat salsa is hardly salsa, as it is laden with preservatives.

So, if you're preparing a full-course Mexican meal, make sure you make your own salsa. In this section we will cover a few of the most popular Mexican sauces and seasonings. Let us dive straight into the recipes!

Achiote Paste (RECADO COLORADO)

This spicy red seasoning is perfect for adding punch to your meat recipes!

Yield: Approximately ¾ Cup

Ingredients:

- ¼ cup olive oil
- ½ cup freshly squeezed lemon juice (about 5 lemons)
- ½ cup freshly squeezed orange juice
- ½ teaspoon whole cloves
- 1 tablespoon black peppercorns
- 10 garlic cloves
- 2 tablespoons salt
- 2 teaspoons cumin seeds

- 3 habanero peppers, seeded
- 5 tablespoons achiote (annatto) seeds
- 8 whole allspice berries

Directions:

1. Use a food processor to pulse-grind the achiote seeds, peppercorns, cumin, allspice, and cloves until thoroughly powdered. Put in the orange juice, habaneros, garlic, and salt and blend until the desired smoothness is achieved. Mix in the lemon juice and olive oil until a paste is achieved.
2. Cover tablespoon-sized portions of the paste using plastic and place it in your freezer for no more than a month.

Ancho and Chile De Árbol Salsa

An insanely delicious rustic salsa from Mexico's interior!

Yield: About 2 cups

Ingredients:

- 1 ancho chile, toasted and rehydrated, 1/3 cup of the soaking water reserved
- 1 teaspoon agave nectar or sugar
- 1 teaspoon salt
- 1 tomato (about 1/2 pound), roasted
- 1/2 cup finely chopped white onion

- 1/2 pound tomatillos, husked and rinsed
- 4 chiles de árbol, toasted and rehydrated

Directions:

1. Put the tomatillos in a small deep cooking pan, submerge them in water, bring them to its boiling point, and simmer until they are tender but not falling apart, about five minutes. Drain and save for later.
2. Finish the salsa. Put the chiles in a blender and put in the reserved 1/3 cup of soaking water. Put in the tomatillos, tomato, agave nectar, and salt to the blender and blend until thoroughly puréed. Pour the salsa into a serving dish and mix in the onions.

Ancho Chile Jam

This jam has a complex sweet & spicy flavour. It can be enjoyed mixed into soups, as a chutney with meat recipes, and much more!

Yield: 2 ½ Cups

Ingredients:

- ½ teaspoon salt
- 2 cloves garlic, peeled
- 2 ounces ancho chiles, approximately 5
- 2 tablespoons honey

- 2 tablespoons white or red wine vinegar
- 6 tablespoons any kind of red jam or jelly

Directions:

1. Use scissors to cut the ancho chiles open, discard the stems, and shake out all the seeds. Put the chiles in a container and add sufficient boiling water to immerse the chiles. Put a small plate on top of the chiles to immerse them. Soak for half an hour, then drain, saving for later 1 cup of the chile soaking water.
2. Put the chiles, garlic, jam, honey, vinegar, and salt in a blender. Put in the 1 cup reserved chile soaking water and pulse on high speed to blend for a minute. Move the jam to an airtight container and place in your fridge for maximum half a year.

Ancho Chile Sauce V2

This delicious spicy sauce goes with pretty much everything!

Yield: Approximately 2½ Cups

Ingredients:

- ¼ cup chopped onion
- ¼ cup raisins
- ½ teaspoon ground cumin
- 1 tablespoon vegetable oil

- 1 teaspoon dried or 1 tablespoon fresh oregano
- 2 ancho chiles
- 2 cups chicken broth
- 2 tomatoes, chopped

Directions:

1. Take the stems and seeds of the chiles and soak them in hot water for about ten minutes. Take the chiles and cut them.
2. In a big deep cooking pan, heat the vegetable oil using high heat. Put in the chiles and onion and sauté until tender, about five minutes. Put in the broth, tomatoes, raisins, oregano, and cumin and bring to its boiling point. Lower the heat and allow to simmer until the tomatoes are cooked, another ten minutes.
3. Cautiously pour all of the contents into a food processor or blender and process until the desired smoothness is achieved. Serve instantly, or store in a firmly sealed container in your fridge for maximum one week.

Arizona-Style Salsa

This salsa from the Mexican state of Sonora goes great with chips or antojitos!

Yield: About 1 cup

Ingredients:

- 1 (8-12 ounce) tomato, roasted
- 1 dried Anaheim (California) chile, or a mild, dried New Mexico chile, toasted and rehydrated
- 1/2 tablespoon rice vinegar
- 1/2 teaspoon salt
- 3 chiles de árbol, toasted and rehydrated

Directions:

1. Throw all ingredients into your blender and pulse for a couple of minutes, or until the desired smoothness is achieved.

Banana Salsa

Tastes great as an appetizer on its own, or as a dip with chips!

Yield: 2 Cups

Ingredients:

- ¼ cup chopped fresh cilantro, leaves and tender stems
- ½ teaspoon salt
- 1 red bell pepper, stemmed and seeded
- 1 serrano chile, thoroughly minced, including the seeds
- 1 whole green onion, minced
- 2 firm yellow skinned bananas
- 2 tablespoons light brown sugar
- 2 tablespoons minced fresh ginger

- 3 tablespoons freshly squeezed lime juice

Directions:

1. Peel the bananas and cut along the length into long strips. Cut across the strips so that the banana is in ½-inch cubes. Mince the red bell pepper and green onion.
2. Mix the bananas with the bell pepper, green onion, cilantro, ginger, chile, lime juice, brown sugar, and salt in a medium container. Press plastic wrap directly across the surface. The salsa can be made twelve hours before serving and placed in the fridge in an airtight container. Allow to reach room temperature and stir before you serve.

BANANA SALSA VARIATION 1: MANGO SALSA

Substitute the bananas with 3 perfectly ripe mangoes. Remove the skin of the mangoes. Cut off the flesh in big pieces, and then cut coarsely to yield 2 to 3 cups. Mix the mango with the rest of the ingredients as directed in the "Banana Salsa" recipe.

BANANA SALSA VARIATION 2: PAPAYA SALSA

Substitute the bananas with 2 firm, underripe Hawaiian papayas or a 3-inch-thick slice of Mexican papaya. Peel, seed, and cut the fruit to yield 2 to 3 cups. Mix the papaya with the rest of the ingredients as directed in the "Banana Salsa" recipe.

BANANA SALSA VARIATION 3: TROPICAL SALSA

Replace the bananas with a mix of chopped fruits— avocado, papaya or mango, strawberries, and kiwi—to yield 2 to 3 cups. Mix the mixed fruit with the rest of the ingredients as directed in the "Banana Salsa" recipe.

BANANA SALSA VARIATION 4: PINEAPPLE SALSA

Replace the bananas with 2 to 3 cups chopped fresh pineapple. Omit the lime juice. Mix the pineapple with the rest of the ingredients as directed in the "Banana Salsa" recipe.

Cebollas En Escabeche (PICKLED ONIONS)

Yield: About 2 cups

An insanely delicious garnish and relish from Yucatán state, this recipe goes great with tacos, seafood, meats, and poultry.

Ingredients:

- 1 (12-ounce) red onion, cut into 1/3-inch rings
- 1 bay leaf
- 1 clove garlic, peeled and smashed
- 1 small habanero chile, cut in half (not necessary)
- 1 teaspoon dried leaf oregano
- 1/2 cup rice vinegar
- 1/2 tablespoon extra-virgin olive oil
- 1/4 cup water
- 1/8 teaspoon salt
- 1/8 teaspoon whole dried thyme

Directions:

1. Make the onions. Put all the ingredients apart from the onion in a big deep cooking pan and simmer for about three minutes.
2. Put the onions in a nonreactive container and pour the hot liquid over them.
3. Allow the onions to sit at room temperature for about two hours, stirring occasionally. Place in your fridge.

Chile Pequín Salsa

Yield: About 1 cup

Don't put too much of this fiery salsa into your mouth in one go. This salsa goes great with steak, seafood, and pork.

Ingredients:

- 1 big or 2 small cloves garlic, minced
- 1 big tomato (approximately eight ounces)
- 1 tablespoon chile pequín
- 1/2 cup chopped white onion
- 1/2 teaspoon rice vinegar
- 1/2 teaspoon salt
- 1/8 teaspoon ground cloves

Directions:

1. Bring sufficient water to cover the tomato to its boiling point and put in the tomato, onion, and garlic. Simmer for about ten minutes, or until the tomato is fairly tender.
2. Peel the tomato and discard the skin. Put the tomato, onion, and garlic in a food processor, put in the rest of the ingredients, and pulse until puréed. Allow about fifteen minutes for the chiles to rehydrate, and process again before you serve.

Chile-Tomatillo Salsa

Poblano chile and tomatillo is an insane combination!

Yield: 2½ Cups

Ingredients:

- ¼ cup packed fresh cilantro, leaves and tender stems

- ½ teaspoon salt
- 1 poblano chile
- 1 serrano chile
- 3 cloves garlic, peeled
- 8 small green tomatillos, husks removed

Directions:

1. In a dry, heavy frying pan on moderate to high heat, mildly char the tomatillos. Char the poblano and rub off the blackened skin. Then discard the seeds and stem. Chop the tomatillos into quarters. In the same dry, heavy frying pan using high heat, mildly brown the garlic and serrano chile. Chop the garlic and chiles a few times so they are in slightly smaller pieces.

2. Put the poblano chile, tomatillos, garlic, serranogarlic mixture (including the seeds), cilantro, and salt in a blender. Blend until the desired smoothness is achieved. If you don't like this method, if you have the time, finely cut the salsa ingredients by hand for a more interesting texture. Taste and calibrate the seasonings for salt. This can be stored for three days refrigerated in an airtight container. Allow to reach room temperature before you serve.

Chimichurri Sauce

Yield: About 3/4 cup

An Argentinian sauce with a Mexican twist! This sauce goes great with meat dishes!

Ingredients:

- 1 tablespoon dried leaf oregano
- 2 teaspoons chile flakes
- 4 teaspoons red wine vinegar
- 6 cloves garlic, very finely chopped or put through a garlic press
- 1/2 cup extra-virgin olive oil
- 1/2 teaspoon salt
- 1/4 cup finely chopped parsley
- 1/4 teaspoon freshly ground black pepper

Directions:

1. Put the olive oil, garlic, oregano, and chile flakes into a small microwave-safe dish and microwave to approximately 135°-150°F on an instant-read thermometer, approximately half a minute on High. You want to heat the garlic just sufficient to release its flavour, but not so much that it actually cooks or makes the oil turn cloudy. Let the oil cool to room temperature.
2. Mix in the vinegar, salt, pepper, and parsley and let the flavours meld for a couple of hours before you serve.

Cranberry-Jalapeño Jelly

Adjust the amount of jalapeño to adjust the hotness of this fiery recipe to your taste!

Yield: 1-1¼ cups

Ingredients:

- 1 cup fresh cranberries
- 1 small jalapeño, stems and seeds removed, very finely chopped
- 1/2 cup sugar
- 1/2 cup water
- 1/4 cup finely chopped dried apricots
- Grated zest from 1/2 orange
- Pinch of salt

Directions:

1. Cook the water and sugar on low-moderate boil for five minutes.
2. Put in the cranberries, apricots, salt, and jalapeño and cook them on low-moderate simmer for about six minutes, at which time the cranberries should be breaking apart. Put in the orange zest and carry on simmering, stirring, until thick, approximately one minute.

Dog's Snout Salsa

A hot and tangy salsa from Yucatán state!

Yield: About 2 cups

Ingredients:

- 1 habanero chile, stemmed, seeded, veins removed, and very finely chopped
- 1/4 cup finely chopped cilantro
- 1/4 heaping teaspoon salt
- 1-1/3 cups chopped tomatoes
- 2/3 cup finely chopped red onion
- 4 tablespoons sour orange juice, or substitute 2 tablespoons freshly squeezed lime juice and 2 tablespoons freshly squeezed orange juice

Directions:

1. Lightly toss together everything apart from the salt. Let the salsa marinate, stirring intermittently, for a couple of hours at room temperature. Mix in the salt before you serve.

Fresh Tomatillo Salsa

This salsa is a bite of pure freshness, and looks absolutely amazing!

Yield: About 1-1/4 cups. Nutrition information is for 1 tablespoon.

Ingredients:

- 1 heaping teaspoon salt
- 1 medium-sized serrano chile, stem removed, finely chopped
- 3 tablespoons chopped cilantro
- 3 tablespoons chopped white onion
- 3/4 pound fresh tomatillos, husked, rinsed, dried, and cut into quarters

Directions:

1. Put all the ingredients in a blender and pulse just until the sauce is dense and lumpy but not thoroughly puréed.

Guacamole

Yield: 2 to 3 Cups

Easily one of the most popular Mexican recipes in the world, Guacamole is easy to prepare, but also just as easy to screw up. The avocado is the most important ingredient in this recipe, so make sure it is fresh and ripe, and preferably Mexican.

Ingredients:

- ½ teaspoon salt
- 1 serrano chile, minced, including the seeds
- 2 cloves garlic, minced
- 2 tablespoons chopped fresh cilantro, leaves and tender stems (not necessary)

- 2 whole green onions, chopped
- 3 ripe avocados
- Freshly squeezed juice of 2 limes

Directions:

1. Chop the avocados in half and remove the pits. Use a spoon to scoop out the flesh. Then purée the avocados using the tongs of a fork. Mix the avocados with the green onions, garlic, chile, cilantro, lime juice, and salt in a medium container. Taste and calibrate the seasonings for salt, lime juice, and chile.
2. If making this more than an hour in advance, squeeze some lime juice over the surface, then secure the surface using plastic wrap. The guacamole will stay perfectly green for a couple of days stored this way in your fridge.

VARIATION

Decorate using crumbled goat cheese, queso fresco, or crema.

Habanero Salsa

An easy to make salsa from Yucatán packing some serious heat.

Yield: About 3/4 cup

Ingredients:

- 1 teaspoon salt
- 1/2 cup cider vinegar

- 1/2 cup pineapple juice
- 4 cloves garlic, unpeeled
- 5 habanero chiles, seeds and veins removed, roughly chopped

Directions:

1. Put the chiles, vinegar, and pineapple juice in a small deep cooking pan, bring to its boiling point, and simmer, covered, for about twelve minutes. Let the liquid and chiles cool.
2. Roast the garlic. Put the garlic in a small frying pan on moderate heat and cook, flipping frequently, until it is slightly charred on the outside and very tender inside, 8-ten minutes. When the garlic is sufficiently cool to handle, peel and roughly cut it.
3. Pour the chiles and their cooking liquid into a blender, put in the garlic and salt, and blend to a purée, approximately one minute. Allow the sauce to cool and the acids to tone down the chile's heat for two to three hours before you serve. Serve with Yucatecan dishes.

Jalisco-Style Pico De Gallo

Famously enjoyed with fajitas all over the world!

Yield: About 3 cups

Ingredients:

- 2 tablespoons freshly squeezed lime juice
- 1/2 cup peeled, seeded, and chopped cucumber, 1/2-inch pieces
- 1/2 cup mango, chopped into 1/2-inch pieces
- 1/2 cup pineapple, chopped into 1/2-inch pieces
- 1/2 cup orange or tangerine segments, cut into 1/2-inch pieces
- 1/2 cup peeled and finely chopped jícama
- 1/2 cup thinly sliced red onion
- 1 teaspoon pure ancho chile powder, or 1/2 teaspoon powder made from chile de árbol
- 1/8 heaping teaspoon salt

Directions:

1. Make the salsa. Mix everything apart from the salt and chile powder.
2. Mix in the salt and chile powder and place in your fridge for thirty minutes to let the flavours blend before you serve.

Manual Salsa Mexicana

This salsa takes time to make, and only works if you have vine-ripened tomatoes on hand.

Yield: 4½ Cups

Ingredients:

- ¼ to ½ cup coarsely chopped fresh cilantro, leaves and tender stems
- ½ teaspoon salt
- 1 to 2 serrano chiles, minced, including the seeds
- 2 whole green onions, minced
- 3 cloves garlic, minced
- 4 cups chopped vine-ripened tomatoes, including skins and seeds

Directions:

1. In a large container, mix the chopped tomatoes with the cilantro, green onions, chiles, garlic, and salt.
2. Taste and calibrate the seasonings, especially for salt and chile flavour. This can be made three days ahead and placed in the fridge in an airtight container.
3. Allow to reach room temperature before you serve.

Mexican Chile Sauce

This sauce tastes insane with grilled meat!

Yield: 3 Cups

Ingredients:

- ¼ cup lightly packed light brown sugar
- ½ teaspoon ground cumin
- ½ teaspoon salt

- 1 serrano chile
- 1 teaspoon dried oregano, or 2 teaspoons minced fresh oregano, preferably Mexican
- 1½ ounces guajillo chiles, approximately 6
- 2 big vine-ripened tomatoes, 12 to 16 ounces
- 4 cloves garlic, peeled

Directions:

1. Chop the stem ends off the guajillo chiles and shake out the seeds. Put the guajillos in a container and cover with boiling water (put a small plate on top of the chiles to immerse them). Soak for half an hour, then drain, saving for later 1 cup of the chile soaking water.
2. Chop the stems off the tomatoes and slice them in half horizontally. Put a dry cast-iron frying pan on moderate to high heat. When hot, mildly brown the garlic, tomatoes, and serrano chile, five minutes. Discard the tomato skins.
3. In a blender, put in the guajillo chiles, garlic, tomato, serrano, brown sugar, cumin, oregano, salt, and the 1 cup reserved chile water. Blend until liquefied. Taste and calibrate the seasonings. This can be stored safely in a fridge for about ninety days stored in an airtight container.

Pasilla Chile Salsa

This salsa goes great with seafood and grilled meat!

Yield: About 2 cups. Nutrition information is for 1 tablespoon.

Ingredients:

- 1 teaspoon canned chipotle chile, or to taste
- 2 teaspoons extra-virgin olive oil, or cooking spray to coat the garlic
- 2 very big pasilla chiles, or 2½ medium to big ones, toasted and rehydrated
- 3 cloves garlic, unpeeled
- 2/3 cup minced white onion
- 1/4 teaspoon dried leaf oregano
- 1-1/4 pounds tomatoes, roasted (about 2 big or 3 medium)
- 3/4 teaspoon salt

Directions:

1. Preheat the oven to 350°F.
2. Brush or spray garlic with some of the olive oil, wrap in foil, and bake until soft, about forty minutes. Peel and reserve the garlic.
3. Combine the ingredients. Put the rehydrated pasilla chiles, the chipotle chile, one of the tomatoes, the oregano, garlic, and salt in a food processor and pulse until a smooth purée is achieved. Put in the rest of the tomato and pulse until it is blended with the other ingredients, but leave the salsa with some texture.
4. Put the rest of the olive oil in a frying pan on moderate heat, put in the onions, and sauté until they are just

starting to become tender. Mix the onions with the rest of the salsa in a container.

Pico De Gallo Salsa

Pico de gallo translates to "beak of the rooster." This recipe is a Mexican favourite and has hundreds of versions. This is probably the most popular version out there. Serve it as a side with tortilla chips!

Yield: 4 Cups

Ingredients:

- ½ medium onion
- 1 jalapeño pepper
- 1 packed cup coarsely chopped fresh cilantro, stems cut
- 1 teaspoon freshly ground black pepper
- 1 teaspoon ground cumin
- 1 teaspoon salt
- 2 garlic cloves
- 2 limes
- 2 pounds Roma or vine-ripened tomatoes

Directions:

1. Cut the tomatoes into little cubes and put them into a large container.

2. Use a food processor to pulse the onion until it is finely chopped (make sure you don't over-process or it'll become gooey). Scrape it into the container with the tomatoes.
3. In the same processor, put in the cilantro and pulse until chopped. Put in to the container with the tomato and onion.
4. Chop the jalapeño in half, along the length, discarding the stem (discard the seeds and veins if you think it'll be too spicy). Pulse the jalapeño and garlic using your processor until thoroughly minced. Scrape into the container with the other vegetables.
5. Chop the limes in half and squeeze their juices into the tomato mixture. Put in the cumin, black pepper, and salt, adding a little extra salt to your taste. Toss together before you serve.

Ranch-Style Salsa (SALSA RANCHERA)

Salsa Ranchera has multiple versions floating around in the world. This version doesn't have an overly strong flavour, and goes great with eggs and meat.

Yield: About 2 cups

Ingredients:

- 1 big guajillo chile, stemmed, seeded, toasted, and rehydrated, 1/2 cup of the soaking water reserved
- 1 clove garlic, minced

- 1 pound tomatoes (about 2 medium to large), roasted
- 1 tablespoon extra-virgin olive oil
- 1/2 teaspoon salt
- 1½ cups chopped white onion

Directions:

1. Combine the tomatoes and chiles. Put the chiles, tomatoes, and the 1/2 cup chile soaking water in a blender and purée thoroughly, a couple of minutes.
2. Heat a big deep cooking pan on moderate heat, put in the oil and onions, and sauté them until they are tender but not browned, about five minutes. Put in the garlic and cook one more minute.
3. Pour the tomatoes and chiles into the deep cooking pan with the onion and garlic and mix in the salt. Bring to a simmer and cook for five to ten minutes, or until the sauce holds together. If it becomes too thick, put in some more water.

Red Enchilada Sauce (SALSA ROJA)

You will never buy enchilada sauce from a store after you make your own!

Yield: 2½ Cups

Ingredients:

- ¼ cup chili powder
- ¼ teaspoon ground cinnamon
- ¼ teaspoon sugar
- ½ teaspoon salt
- 1 tablespoon flour
- 1 teaspoon dried or 1 tablespoon chopped fresh oregano
- 1 teaspoon ground cumin
- 2 cups chicken broth
- 3 tablespoons garlic powder
- 3 tablespoons vegetable oil
- Two 5-ounce cans tomato sauce

Directions:

1. Heat the vegetable oil in a moderate-sized deep cooking pan on moderate heat. Put in the flour and stir, smoothing it out to make a roux, and cook for about one minute. Put in the chili powder and cook for an additional half a minute. Put in the broth, tomato sauce, garlic powder, oregano, cumin, salt, sugar, and cinnamon and stir until blended.
2. Raise the heat and bring to its boiling point, then decrease the heat to moderate and cook until the flavours deepen, an additional fifteen minutes.
3. Turn off the heat and use in your favorite enchilada recipe, pour over burritos to make them "wet," or to make tamales. If you're not using the sauce immediately, store it

in a glass jar with a firmly fitting lid in your fridge for maximum one week.

ROASTED TOMATILLO SALSA (SALSA VERDE)

One of the most popular tomato-bases salsa out there!

Yield: 3 Cups

Ingredients:

- 1 bunch fresh cilantro, stems cut
- 1 jalapeño, stemmed and halved
- 1 small (or ½ medium) onion, quartered
- 1 teaspoon salt
- 1½ pounds (12 to 15) tomatillos, husked and washed
- 4 or 5 garlic cloves

Directions:

1. Preheat your broiler.
2. Chop the tomatillos in half and place them, cut-sides down, on a foil-lined baking sheet. Put under a broiler until the skins are fairly blackened on top, about eight to ten minutes.

3. Cautiously pierce the tomatillos using a fork and put them in a food processor or blender. Put in the onion and garlic and pulse until blended. Put in the cilantro, jalapeño, and salt and pulse until puréed.
4. Go ahead; taste it before you serve and add a little extra salt, if required.

Roasted-Tomato and Pumpkin Seed Salsa

A simple and delicious salsa that tastes insane with grilled meat!

Yield: About 2½ cups

Ingredients:

- 1 medium to big serrano chile
- 1 teaspoon salt, or to taste
- 1/2 cup toasted and ground pumpkin seeds (pepitas) (from 2/3 cup raw hulled pumpkin seeds)
- 1/2-inch slice of white onion
- 2 cloves garlic, peeled
- 3 or 4 tomatoes, for a total of about 1½ pounds

Directions:

1. Put the tomatoes and chile on a baking sheet as close to your broiler as possible and broil until the tomatoes have become tender and barely start to char, about ten to fifteen minutes. Put in the onion and garlic and carry on

cooking until the onion is slightly charred and the garlic is soft, an additional five to ten minutes. Ensure that the tomatoes are thoroughly cooked and fairly tender. Take the vegetables out of the oven, put them in a food processor, put in the salt, and pulse until the sauce is smooth.

2. As the vegetables broil, heat a nonstick frying pan on moderate heat and toast the pumpkin seeds, stirring regularly, until most of them have popped. Don't allow them to scorch. Grind the toasted seeds to a powder in a spice or coffee grinder. Put in 1/2 cup of the ground seeds and the salt to the processor and pulse with the other ingredients until everything is well blended.

Romesco Sauce

Insanely nutritious and delicious, this sauce goes with pretty much everything.

Yield: About 1 cup

Ingredients:

- 1 cup cherry tomatoes
- 1 small to moderate canned chipotle chile, seeded and chopped
- 1 tablespoon sherry vinegar (or freshly squeezed lime or lemon juice)
- 1/2 heaping teaspoon salt

- 1/2 teaspoon sweet smoked Spanish paprika
- 1/3 cup extra-virgin olive oil
- 2 tablespoons minced parsley
- 2 tablespoons roasted and skinned whole almonds
- 3 garlic cloves, peeled and cut in half along the length

Directions:

1. Dry roast the tomatoes, nuts, and garlic. Heat an ungreased frying pan on moderate to high heat until it is very hot. Put the tomatoes, almonds, and garlic in the frying pan and cook, stirring continuously, until the tomatoes are blackened and just beginning to deflate. It is okay if the nuts and garlic seem burned; that just augments the flavour. Do make sure that the garlic is thoroughly cooked.
2. Finish the sauce. Put the tomatoes, almonds, and garlic in a food processor, put in the rest of the ingredients, and process in pulses until the sauce is thick but still has some texture.

Salsa De Chile (Chile Sauce)

One of the most versatile salsa recipes in this book, chile sauce will go with pretty much everything.

Yield: About 2½ cups

Ingredients:

- 1 tablespoon extra-virgin olive oil
- 1 teaspoon dried leaf oregano
- 1 teaspoon rice vinegar
- 2 bay leaves
- 3/4 teaspoon salt, or to taste
- 4 cloves garlic, chopped
- 8 mild to moderate-hot New Mexico dried red chiles, 12 guajillo chiles, or 4 medium-sized ancho chiles, stemmed, seeded, toasted, and rehydrated, 4 cups soaking water reserved

Directions:

1. Combine the sauce ingredients. Put the chiles in a blender, put in the garlic, oregano, and 2 cups of the reserved chile soaking water, and blend for a couple of minutes, or until comprehensively puréed. Put in the rest of the 2 cups chile soaking water and blend one more minute.
2. Cook the sauce. Heat a big deep cooking pan on moderate heat, put in the olive oil, and mix in the blended sauce ingredients. Put in the vinegar and bay leaves, bring to its boiling point, and cook on a moderate simmer until the sauce is barely sufficiently thick to coat the back of a spoon, or the consistency of a very thin milkshake, about fifteen minutes. If the sauce becomes too thick, put in some more water. If it is too thin, cook it a bit longer. Put in the salt and simmer one more minute.

Salsa De Molcajete

A traditional Mexican salsa. Salsa doesn't get more authentic than this!

Yield: About 1 cup

Ingredients:

- 1 chile de árbol, toasted in an oil-filmed frying pan until crisp but not burned
- 1 small jalapeño chile, roasted and peeled
- 1 tomato, broiled and peeled
- 1 very small pasilla chile, toasted in an oil-filmed frying pan until crisp but not burned
- 2 chiles pequín, toasted in an oil-filmed frying pan until crisp but not burned
- 2 cloves garlic
- 2 tablespoons finely chopped white onion
- 2 teaspoons toasted sesame seeds
- 2/3 of 1 small ancho chile, toasted in an oil-filmed frying pan until crisp but not burned
- 3/4 teaspoon salt
- Water as needed to get the consistency you want

Directions:

1. Put in the salt to the molcajete.
2. Put in the ingredients one at a time, grinding each one to the texture you want before you put in the next.

Salsa Fresca

A great all-round salsa!

Yield: About 1 cup

Ingredients:

- 1/2 teaspoon salt
- 1/4-ounce serrano chile (about 1-1/4 inches) long, cut into 1/3-inch pieces
- 1/4 cup loosely packed, roughly chopped cilantro
- 1/4 cup very finely chopped white onion
- 1/4 cup water (not necessary)
- 4 ounces tomatillos, husked, rinsed, dried, and cut into 3/4-inch pieces
- 6 ounces Roma tomatoes, cut into 3/4-inch pieces

Directions:

1. If you have a meat grinder, grind together into a container the tomatillos, tomatoes, chile, and cilantro.
2. Mix in the onion and salt. If you are using a food processor, put the tomatillos, tomatoes, chile, and cilantro into the work container, put in 1/4 cup water, and pulse until everything is finely chopped (as if it had been put through a meat grinder).
3. Mix in the onions and salt.

Smoky Chipotle Salsa (SALSA CON CHIPOTLE)

This moderately spicy salsa tastes great with a side of chips.

Yield: Approximately 5 Cups

Ingredients:

- ½ teaspoon freshly ground black pepper
- 1 onion, chopped
- 12 garlic cloves, sliced
- 2 tablespoons freshly squeezed lime juice
- 2 tablespoons olive oil
- 2 tablespoons salt
- 3 cups chipotle peppers in adobo sauce
- 8 Roma tomatoes, coarsely chopped

Directions:

1. Heat the olive oil in a big frying pan using high heat. Put in the garlic and onion and allow them to brown, stirring only a couple of times (about 2 minutes). Put in the chipotle with adobo sauce and the tomatoes and cook for another three to four minutes until thoroughly heated.
2. Cautiously pour the mixture into a blender or food processor. Put in the salt, lime juice, and black pepper and blend until the desired smoothness is achieved.
3. Serve instantly or save it in your fridge for a few days.

Tangerine-Serrano Salsa

Are tangerines in season? This is the salsa to try!

Yield: 3 to 4 Cups

Ingredients:

- ¼ cup chopped fresh cilantro, leaves and tender stems
- ¼ cup freshly squeezed lime juice
- ¼ cup lightly packed light brown sugar
- ½ cup chopped red onion
- ½ teaspoon salt
- 1 serrano chile, minced, including the seeds
- 1 tablespoon finely grated tangerine zest
- 2 tablespoons minced fresh ginger
- 3 cloves garlic, minced
- 4 tangerines, peeled, segments separated and chopped

Directions:

1. Mix the tangerine zest and segments, onion, cilantro, chile, garlic, ginger, lime juice, brown sugar, and salt in a medium container.
2. This can be made one day in advance and placed in the fridge in an airtight container. Allow to reach room temperature before you serve.

The Ultimate Mojo De Ajo Sauce

Mojo de ajo (garlic sauce) is enjoyed with seafood all over Mexico.

Yield: About 3/4 cup. Nutrition information is for 1 tablespoon.

Ingredients:

- 1½ tablespoons dried cilantro
- 3 chiles de árbol, seeded and coarsely chopped, or substitute a finely chopped canned chipotle chile
- 4 sun-dried tomatoes (not packed in oil), very finely chopped
- 1/2 cup extra-virgin olive oil
- 1/2 tablespoon freshly squeezed lime juice
- 1/2 teaspoon salt
- 1/4 cup minced white onion
- 1/4 heaping teaspoon freshly ground black pepper
- 1/4 cup garlic chopped into 1/8-inch or slightly larger pieces

Directions:

1. Make the sauce. Put the chiles, tomatoes, garlic, onion, salt, oil, and pepper in a small deep cooking pan on moderate to low heat and cook until the oil just starts to bubble. Keep adjusting the heat so that the mixture cooks at the barest simmer, with just a few bubbles.
2. Cook until the garlic is very tender and just starting to brown, about forty minutes, stirring every five minutes or so. Put in the cilantro and lime juice and simmer an

additional ten minutes, or until the garlic just starts to take on a golden hue.

Watermelon Relish

A refreshing, crunchy, and spicy relish!

Yield: 3 Cups

Ingredients:

- ¼ cup freshly squeezed lime juice
- ¼ cup lightly packed light brown sugar
- ½ serrano chile, minced, including the seeds
- ½ teaspoon salt
- 2 tablespoons chopped fresh cilantro, leaves and tender stems
- 2 tablespoons chopped fresh mint leaves
- 2 tablespoons minced fresh ginger
- 3 pounds seedless red watermelon

Directions:

1. Remove all the rind from the melon and chop the melon into ½-inch cubes. You should have about 6 cups. Put 4 cups of the watermelon in a blender. Put in the ginger, chile, lime juice, brown sugar, and salt. liquefied. Move to a big deep cooking pan. Bring to a rapid boil on moderate

to high heat and boil until reduced to 1 cup. Move to a container and let cool to room temperature.

2. Mix in the rest of the 2 cups chopped watermelon, the cilantro, and mint. This can be made 2 days ahead and placed in the fridge in an airtight container. Serve at room temperature.

Yucatán-Style Tomato Salsa

A tomato salsa spiced up with habanero chiles!

Yield: About 1-1/4 cups

Ingredients:

- 1 habanero chile, cut in half
- 1 pound (about 2 medium-sized) tomatoes
- 1/2 cup chopped white onion
- 1/8 heaping teaspoon salt
- 1½ tablespoons extra-virgin olive oil
- 2½ cups water

Directions:

1. Bring the water to its boiling point and put in the tomatoes and chiles. Simmer for about four minutes, or until the tomatoes are starting to become tender. Take the tomatoes and chiles from the pan; let the tomatoes cool down a little then remove and discard their skins and put

the tomatoes in a food processor with the steel blade. Reserve the cooking liquid for a future cook. Reserve the chiles separately.

2. Cook the onions and purée the sauce. Heat a frying pan on moderate heat, put in 1/2 tablespoon of the oil and the onions, and sauté, stirring regularly, until the onions barely start to turn golden. Put the onions in the food processor with the tomatoes and process for a minute. Put the sauce through a strainer or food mill to remove the seeds.

3. Cook the tomato sauce. Heat a small deep cooking pan on moderate heat, put in the rest of the tablespoon oil, the sauce, and the salt. If you think the sauce needs more heat, put in back the habanero halves. Bring the sauce to its boiling point and simmer until it is thick enoigh to hold its shape, about three minutes. If you used the chiles, remove and discard them.

Three Zigzag Sauces

Here are three amazing Mexican sauces that are more versatile than a swiss knife. These are commonly used to garnish dishes, topping them in a zig-zag manner. What you do with these is completely up to you!

Chipotle Chile Zigzag Sauce

Yield: ¾ Cup

Ingredients:

- ¼ teaspoon salt
- ½ cup crema, mayonnaise, or sour cream
- 1 chipotle chile in adobo sauce, minced
- 1 clove garlic, minced
- 1 tablespoon freshly squeezed lime juice
- 2 teaspoons finely grated lime zest

Directions:

1. Mix all of the ingredients together in a small container or an electric mini-chop.
2. Store in your fridge in an airtight container and use within one week.

Cilantro Zigzag Sauce

Yield: ¾ Cup

Ingredients:

- ¼ teaspoon salt
- ½ cup crema, mayonnaise, or sour cream
- ½ cup fresh cilantro, leaves and tender stems
- 1 tablespoon freshly squeezed lime juice
- 1 tablespoon thoroughly minced fresh ginger

Directions:

1. Mix all of the ingredients together in a small container or an electric mini-chop.
2. Store in your fridge in an airtight container and use within one week.

Orange-Ginger Zigzag Sauce

Yield: 1 Cup

Ingredients:

- ½ cup crema, mayonnaise, or sour cream
- ½ serrano chile, minced, including the seeds
- ½ teaspoon finely grated orange zest
- ½ teaspoon salt
- 1 clove garlic, minced
- 1 tablespoon freshly squeezed lime juice
- 1 tablespoon Grand Marnier
- 2 tablespoons chopped fresh mint leaves or cilantro leaves and tender stems
- 2 tablespoons minced fresh ginger
- 2 teaspoons Worcestershire sauce

Directions:

1. Mix all of the ingredients together in a small container or an electric mini-chop.
2. Store in your fridge in an airtight container and use within one week.

OTHER MEXICAN SEASONINGS

All-Purpose Marinade for Chicken, Pork, and Seafood

Rub this all over your meat before you cook, and enjoy the ultimate Mexican flavour!

Yield: ½ Cup

Ingredients:

- ¼ cup extra-virgin olive oil
- ½ teaspoon salt
- 1 tablespoon freshly ground black pepper
- 1 teaspoon ground cinnamon, preferably Mexican
- 1 teaspoon ground coriander or cumin
- 2 teaspoons finely grated lime zest
- 2 teaspoons finely grated orange zest

Directions:

1. Mix the pepper, zests, coriander, cinnamon, and salt in a small container.
2. Rub the spice blend over the surface of the meat or seafood.
3. Next, rub the olive oil over the entire surface as well.
4. Proceed with grilling or roasting, as desired.

Refried Beans

These are a Mexican staple that can be used to give texture and flavour to main course meals.

Yield: 2 Cups

Ingredients:

- ½ teaspoon salt
- 1 cup dried black beans
- 1 medium yellow onion, diced
- 2 cloves garlic, minced
- 3 tablespoons lard

Directions:

1. Spread the beans on a plate and pick through the beans to remove any pebbles. Rinse the beans, then cover with cold water and soak overnight.
2. Drain the beans and put in to a deep cooking pan. Put in 4 cups hot water to the soaked beans. Simmer on moderate heat until tender, approximately 1½ hours. Remove and reserve 2 cups of the cooking water. If you don't like this method, follow the quick-cooking directions on the bean package.
3. In a big frying pan, melt the lard on moderate heat. Put in the onion and cook until the onion becomes golden, approximately ten minutes. Put in the garlic and cook for 1 more minute. Put in the salt and beans. Mash the beans

using a fork, adding just sufficient of the reserved cooking water to make the beans smooth. If you don't like this method, put in a food processor and process until the desired smoothness is achieved. The beans can be made up to four days in advance. Let cool and then place in your fridge in an airtight container.

DRY RUBS

These dry rubs are great on any meat that can be grilled or oven-roasted. Each rub makes about 6 tablespoons, sufficient to season 8 of your favorite steaks, or 8 chicken breasts, or 3 pounds of fish. Just rub the dry rub into the surface of the meat or seafood, then rub the meat with extra-virgin olive oil. As another option, after rubbing the meat with the dry rub, we like to rub the meat with Chinese mushroom soy sauce or Chinese dark soy sauce. This is not authentic Mexican, but it is delicious! Remember, the rub has to be massaged with vigor into the meat fibers. Then when you brush the meat with a marinade or olive oil before cooking, the rub will not dislodge from the meat during grilling.

ANCHO DRY RUB

Yield: Approximately 6 TABLESPOONS

Ingredients:

- ¼ cup lightly packed light brown sugar
- 1 (2-inch) cinnamon stick, preferably Mexican
- 1 tablespoon ancho or chipotle chile powder
- 1 tablespoon coriander seeds

Directions:

1. Put all of the ingredients in a clean electric coffee grinder or spice grinder. Grind into a fine powder.
2. Move to an empty glass spice jar, label, and store in your spice rack for maximum half a year.

CARAWAY DRY RUB

Yield: Approximately 6 TABLESPOONS

Ingredients:

- 1 (1-inch) cinnamon stick, preferably Mexican
- 1 tablespoon caraway seeds
- 1 tablespoon coriander seeds
- 1 tablespoon crushed red pepper
- 1 tablespoon cumin seeds
- 1 tablespoon salt
- 1 teaspoon whole cloves

Directions:

1. Put all of the ingredients in a clean electric coffee grinder or spice grinder. Grind into a fine powder.

2. Move to an empty glass spice jar, label, and store in your spice rack for maximum half a year.

ESPRESSO DRY RUB

Yield: Approximately 6 TABLESPOONS

Ingredients:

- 1 tablespoon coriander seeds
- 1 tablespoon crushed red pepper
- 1 tablespoon curry powder
- 1 tablespoon espresso powder
- 1 tablespoon rainbow peppercorn mix
- 1 tablespoon salt

Directions:

1. Put all of the ingredients in a clean electric coffee grinder or spice grinder. Grind into a fine powder.
2. Move to an empty glass spice jar, label, and store in your spice rack for maximum half a year.

APPETIZERS AND DRINKS

Mexicans love appetizers to nibble on, simply because there are so many awesome appetizers available to them to nibble on.

FLAMED CHEESE (QUESO FLAMEADO)

Yield: Servings 6

This robust mexican version of a cheese fondue is best served with picante tomato sauce and a stack of flour tortillas.

Ingredients:

- 1½ dozen flour tortillas
- 12 ounces (340 g) chihuahua cheese or muenster, thinly cut
- 6 ounces (180 g) mexican chorizos, skinned, crumbled, and fried (not necessary)

Directions:

1. Put the cheese in two layers in a shallow, flameproof dish.
2. Melt the cheese either on top of the stove or in your oven, drizzling the chorizo over it.
3. Heat the tortillas and serve instantly, with the sauce on the side.

FRIED PUMPKIN (CALABAZA FRITA)

Yield: about 5 cups (1.25 l)

A delicious recipe for all pumpkin lovers out there!

Ingredients:

- ⅓ to ½ cup (85 to 125 ml) olive oil (not extra virgin)
- 1 green pepper, seeded and finely chopped (1 scant cup/235 ml)
- 1 small white onion, finely chopped (½ cup/125 ml)
- 12 ounces (340 g) tomatoes, finely chopped (about 2 cups/500 ml)
- 2 pounds (900 g) unpeeled pumpkin, cut into little pieces
- Salt to taste

To serve

- ⅓ cup (85 ml) finely grated queso seco de chiapas or añejo or romano cheese

Directions:

1. Place the pumpkin pieces into a big pot, cover with water, bring to its boiling point, reduce the heat, and cook, covered, until still slightly firm, approximately twenty minutes depending on the kind of pumpkin. Drain, peel, and slice into ½-inch (1.5-cm) cubes. Set aside.
2. Heat the oil in a deep flameproof casserole; put in the onion, pepper, and tomatoes with salt to taste and cook

on moderate heat, stirring occasionally to prevent sticking, until well seasoned and still slightly juicy—approximately eight minutes.

3. Put in the cubed pumpkin and mix thoroughly. Carry on cooking over low heat while stirring occasionally to prevent sticking, putting in a little water if mixture is too dry, for approximately fifteen minutes. Examine for salt, then set aside to season for minimum 30 minutes.

4. Serve sprinkled with the cheese and accompanied by tostadas.

7 LAYER DIP

Yield: Servings 8 to 10

Although not a traditional Mexican dish, this recipe is loaded with Mexican ingredients, and make a great appetizer!

Ingredients:

- ¾ teaspoon chili powder
- 1 (fifteen ounce) can black beans, drained but not washed
- 1 pound pepper Jack cheese, shredded (4 cups)
- 1 recipe (3 cups) Chunky Guacamole
- 1½ cups sour cream
- 2 garlic cloves, minced
- 2 jalapeño chiles, stemmed, seeded, and minced
- 2 tablespoons plus 2 teaspoons lime juice (2 limes)

- 3 tablespoons minced fresh cilantro
- 4 big tomatoes, cored, seeded, and chopped fine
- 6 scallions (2 minced; 4, green parts only, cut thin)
- Salt

Directions:

1. Mix tomatoes, minced scallions, jala peños, cilantro, 2 tablespoons lime juice, and ⅛ teaspoon salt in container. Allow to sit until tomatoes start to tenderize, approximately 30 minutes. Drain mixture, discard liquid, and return to container.

2. In the meantime, pulse beans, garlic, chili powder, remaining 2 teaspoons lime juice, and ⅛ teaspoon salt in food processor to crude paste, approximately fifteen pulses. Spread bean mixture uniformly into 8 inch square baking dish or 1 quart glass container.

3. In clean, dry workbowl, pulse 2½ cups pepper Jack and sour cream until the desired smoothness is achieved, approximately fifteen pulses. Spread sour cream mixture uniformly over bean layer. Top uniformly with remaining 1½ cups pepper Jack, followed by guacamole and, finally, drained tomato mixture. (Immerse can be placed in your fridge for maximum one day; bring to room temperature before you serve.) Drizzle with cut scallion greens before you serve.

AGUAS FRESCAS

Yield: 8 cups; serves 8 to 10

These delicious non-alcoholic beverages are usually made by blending fruits, grains, seeds, or flowers with sugar and water.

HIBISCUS AGUA FRESCA

Keep the flowers placed in the fridge in an airtight container.

Ingredients:

- 1 cup sugar
- 2 cups dried hibiscus flowers, washed
- 8 cups water
- Pinch salt

Directions:

1. Bring 4 cups water to boil in medium deep cooking pan. Off heat, mix in hibiscus flowers, cover, and allow to steep for an hour. Strain mixture into 2 quart pitcher; discard solids.
2. Mix in sugar and salt until blended, then mix in remaining 4 cups water.
3. Place in your fridge until completely chilled, approximately 2 hours. Serve over ice. (Agua Fresca can be placed in your fridge for maximum 5 days; stir to remix before you serve.)

WATERMELON LIME AGUA FRESCA

If you can't find seedless watermelon, remove as many seeds as you can before processing.

Ingredients:

- ⅛ teaspoon salt
- ⅓ cup lime juice (3 limes), plus extra as required
- 2 cups water
- 2 tablespoons agave nectar or honey, as required
- 8 cups seedless watermelon, cut into an inch pieces
- Mint leaves (not necessary)

Directions:

1. Working in 2 batches, process watermelon and water in blender until the desired smoothness is achieved, approximately half a minute.
2. Strain mixture through fine mesh strainer into 2 quart pitcher; discard solids. Mix in lime juice, agave, and salt into watermelon mixture. Mix in extra lime juice and agave to taste.
3. Serve over ice with mint, if using. (Agua Fresca can be placed in your fridge for maximum 5 days; stir to remix before you serve.)

BEAN AND BEEF TAQUITOS

Yield: Servings four to 6

These large tortillas taste absolutely amazing with Avocado Sauce!

Ingredients:

- ½ cup water
- 1 (8 ounce) can tomato sauce
- 1 big egg, lightly beaten
- 1 cup canned pinto beans, washed
- 1 cup plus 4 teaspoons vegetable oil
- 1 onion, halved and cut thin
- 1 teaspoon chili powder
- 1 teaspoon ground cumin
- 12 (6 inch) corn tortillas
- 2 jalapeño chiles, stemmed, seeded, and minced
- 3 garlic cloves, minced
- 3 tablespoons minced fresh cilantro
- 8 ounces 90 percent lean ground beef
- Salt and pepper

Directions:

1. Heat 1 teaspoon oil in 12 inch nonstick frying pan over moderate high heat until just smoking. Put in ground beef and cook, breaking up meat with wooden spoon, until no longer pink, approximately five minutes. Drain beef in colander. In separate container, purée beans to paste with potato masher.

2. Heat 1 tablespoon oil in now empty frying pan on moderate heat until shimmering. Put in onion and cook until tender and mildly browned, five to seven minutes. Mix in jalapeños, garlic, cumin, and chili powder and cook until aromatic, approximately half a minute. Mix in tomato sauce, water, cilantro, ½ teaspoon salt, ½ teaspoon pepper, drained beef, and mashed beans. Cook while stirring frequently, until mixture has thickened and starts to sizzle, approximately ten minutes. Sprinkle with salt and pepper to taste, move to container, and allow to cool for about twenty minutes.

3. Adjust oven rack to middle position and heat oven to 200 degrees. Coat rimmed baking sheet using parchment paper. Set wire rack in second rimmed baking sheet. Stack 6 tortillas, wrap in damp dish towel, and place on plate; microwave until warm and flexible, approximately one minute.

4. Working with one tortilla at a time, brush edges of top half with beaten egg. Spread 3 tablespoons filling in tight row across lower half of tortilla, fold bottom of tortilla over filling, then pull back on tortilla to tighten around filling. Roll firmly, place seam side down on parchment covered sheet, and cover with second damp towel. Microwave remaining 6 tortillas and repeat with rest of the filling. (Taquitos can be covered with damp towel, wrapped firmly using plastic wrap, and placed in the fridge for maximum one day.)

5. Put in remaining 1 cup oil to clean, dry 12 inch nonstick frying pan and heat over moderate high heat to 350 degrees. Using tongs, place 6 taquitos, seam side down, in oil. Fry taquitos until golden on all sides, approximately eight minutes, turning as required and adjusting heat as required to maintain oil temperature between 300 and 325 degrees. Move to prepared wire rack and place in oven to keep warm while repeating with remaining 6 taquitos and serve.

BLACK BEAN DIP

Yield: about 2 cups

Black beans are a staple in the Mexican kitchen, and can be use to make some insanely delicious and smooth dips, such as this one.

Ingredients:

- ½ onion, chopped
- ½ teaspoon ground cumin
- 1 garlic clove, minced
- 1 tablespoon extra virgin olive oil
- 1 teaspoon minced canned chipotle chile in adobo sauce
- 1 teaspoon minced fresh oregano
- 2 (fifteen ounce) cans black beans, washed
- 2 tablespoons lime juice

- 2 tablespoons minced fresh cilantro
- Salt

Directions:

1. Mix lime juice, garlic, and oregano in small container; set aside for minimum fifteen minutes.
2. Pulse beans, onion, oil, chipotle, cumin, ¼ teaspoon salt, and lime juice mixture in food processor until fully ground, 5 to 10 pulses. Scrape down sides of container with rubber spatula. Continue to pulse until uniform paste forms, approximately 1 minute, scraping down container a couple of times.
3. Move dip to container, cover, and allow it to sit at room temperature for minimum 30 minutes. (Immerse can be placed in your fridge for maximum one day; bring to room temperature before you serve.) Mix in cilantro and sprinkle with salt to taste before you serve.

CHILE-SEASONED PORK (CHILORIO)

Yield: enough to fill twelve tortillas

Ingredients:

- ⅛ teaspoon cumin seeds, crushed
- ¼ teaspoon dried mexican oregano
- ⅓ cup (85 ml) mild vinegar; make up to ½ cup (125 ml) of liquid by putting in water

- 2 pounds (900 g) pork shoulder, without bone but with some fat
- 2 teaspoons salt
- 8 ancho chiles, seeds and veins removed
- 8 garlic cloves, roughly chopped
- Lard as required
- Salt to taste

Directions:

1. Chop the meat into 1-inch (2.5-cm) cubes and cook with salt as for carnitas. When the water has vaporized and the fat has rendered out of the meat but the meat hasn't browned—about forty-five minutes—take the meat out of the dish and pound it in the molcajete until it is completely shredded, or shred it finely using two forks.
2. In the meantime, make the sauce. Cover the chiles with hot water. Soak for about ten minutes and drain.
3. Place the diluted vinegar into your blender jar with the garlic and spices and blend as smooth as you can. Slowly put in the chiles and blend after each addition. The sauce must be thick, more like a paste. You will have to keep stopping the blender to release the blades. Only put in more liquid if required to release the blades of the blender.
4. There must be about ¼ cup (65 ml) of fat in the dish in which the meat was cooked; if not, make up to that amount with lard. Put in the meat and blend the chile

sauce thoroughly into it. Cook using low heat for fifteen to twenty minutes, or until the meat is well seasoned and the mixture rather dry, scraping the bottom of the dish to prevent sticking.

5. Chilorio will keep for months in your fridge.

CHILIED PEANUTS (CACAHUATES ENCHILADOS)

Yield: approximately 1 cup (250 ml)

These fiery little snacks are commonly enjoyed in Mexican bars with tequila.

Ingredients:

- 1 cup (250 ml) raw shelled peanuts, with or without brown papery skins
- 1 tablespoon vegetable oil
- 1 teaspoon salt, or to taste
- 1 to 1½ teaspoons powdered chile de árbol, or to taste
- 10 small garlic cloves

Directions:

1. In a frying pan just big enough to accommodate the peanuts in a single layer, heat the oil. Put in the peanuts and garlic cloves and fry for approximately 2 minutes, flipping them over continuously.

2. Reduce the heat a little, put in the powdered chile and salt, and cook for one minute or two longer, stirring occasionally to prevent sticking; take care that the chile powder does not burn.
3. Set aside to cool before you serve with drinks.

CHUNKY GUACAMOLE

Yield: about 3 cups

A chunky version of the classic guacamole which goes great with homemade chips!

Ingredients:

- ¼ cup minced fresh cilantro
- ½ teaspoon ground cumin
- 1 jalapeño chile, stemmed, seeded, and minced
- 2 garlic cloves, minced
- 2 tablespoons finely chopped red onion
- 2 tablespoons lime juice
- 3 ripe avocados
- Salt

Directions:

1. Halve 1 avocado, remove pit, and scoop flesh into moderate container. Put in cilantro, jalapeño, onion, lime

juice, garlic, ¾ teaspoon salt, and cumin and purée with potato masher (or fork) until mostly smooth.

2. Halve, pit, and dice remaining 2 avocados. Put in cubes to container with mashed avocado mixture and gently purée until mixture is well blended but still coarse. (Guacamole can be placed in your fridge for maximum one day using plastic wrap pressed directly against its surface.) Sprinkle with salt to taste before you serve.

DRIED SHRIMP FRITTERS (BOTANAS DE CAMARÓN SECO)

Yield: about 24 botanas

Ingredients:

- ½ cup (125 ml) finely chopped white onion
- ¾ cup (190 ml) small dried shrimps, cleaned
- 1 cup (250 ml) cold water
- 1 egg white
- 4 ounces (115 g) flour (approximately 1 scant cup)
- 5 serrano chiles, finely chopped
- Salt to taste
- Vegetable oil for frying

Directions:

1. Combine the flour, water, and salt together for a couple of minutes and leave the batter to stand for minimum 1 hour.
2. Wash the shrimps to remove surplus salt. Cover with warm water and leave them to soak for approximately five minutes—no longer.
3. Beat the egg white until stiff and fold it into the batter.
4. Drain the shrimps (if large, cut into 2) and put in them, with the chopped onion and chiles, to the batter.
5. Heat the oil in a frying pan and drop tablespoons of the mixture into it, a few at a time. Fry the botanas until they become golden brown, flipping them over once. Drain them on the paper towelling and serve instantly.

EMPANADAS

Yield: 24 empanadas

These filled pastries are a quite popular all over Mexico.

Ingredients:

- 1 recipe filling, chilled
- 1 tablespoon sugar
- 1¼ cups ice water
- 1½ teaspoons salt
- 12 tablespoons unsalted butter, cut into ½ inch pieces and chilled
- 2 tablespoons extra virgin olive oil

- 3¾ cups (18¾ ounces) all-purpose flour

Directions:

1. Process flour, sugar, and salt together in food processor until blended, approximately 3 seconds. Spread butter pieces over flour mixture and pulse until mixture resembles coarse cornmeal, approximately 16 pulses. Move mixture to big container. Working with ¼ cup ice water at a time, drizzle water over flour mixture and, using stiff rubber spatula, stir and press dough together until dough sticks together and no small bits of flour remain (you may not need to use all of water).

2. Turn dough onto clean, dry counter and softly push into consistent ball. Split dough into 2 even pieces. Turn each piece of dough onto sheet of plastic wrap, flatten into 6 inch disks, wrap firmly, and place in your fridge for an hour. Allow the chilled dough to sit on counter to tenderize slightly, approximately ten minutes, before rolling.

3. Adjust oven racks to upper middle and lower middle positions and heat oven to 425 degrees. Coat 2 baking sheets using parchment paper. Roll 1 dough disk into 18 inch circle, approximately ⅛ inch thick, on mildly floured counter. Using 4 inch round biscuit cutter, cut out 12 rounds, discarding dough scraps. Put 1 tablespoon filling in center of each dough round. Brush edges of dough with water and fold dough over filling. Push to secure, and

crimp edges with tines of fork. Move to 1 prepared sheet, cover, and place in your fridge Repeat with the rest of the dough disk and rest of the filling. (Filled empanadas can be wrapped firmly using plastic wrap and placed in the fridge for maximum one day or frozen for maximum 1 month. After empanadas are completely frozen, approximately eight hours, they can be moved to zipper lock freezer bags to save space in freezer. Move back to parchment paper covered sheet before you bake. Increase baking time by about five minutes.)

4. Brush tops of empanadas with oil and bake until a golden-brown colour is achieved, twenty minutes to half an hour, switching and rotating sheets midway through baking. Allow to cool for five minutes before you serve.

EMPANADA FILLINGS

These fillings should be chilled at the time of using, and hence should be prepared in advance. Each filling makes enough for 24 empanadas.

BEEF AND CHEESE FILLING

Ingredients:

- ⅛ teaspoon cayenne pepper
- ⅛ teaspoon ground cloves
- ½ cup beef broth
- 1 onion, chopped fine
- 1 tablespoon extra virgin olive oil

- 1 tablespoon tomato paste
- 1 teaspoon ground cumin
- 1 teaspoon minced fresh oregano or ¼ teaspoon dried
- 12 ounces 85 percent lean ground beef
- 2 tablespoons minced fresh cilantro
- 3 garlic cloves, minced
- 4 ounces Monterey Jack cheese, shredded (1 cup)
- Salt and pepper

Directions:

1. Heat oil in 12 inch frying pan on moderate heat until just shimmering. Put in onion and cook until tender, approximately five minutes.
2. Mix in garlic, tomato paste, oregano, cumin, clove, and cayenne and cook until aromatic, approximately one minute.
3. Put in ground beef and cook, breaking up meat with wooden spoon, until beef is no longer pink, approximately five minutes.
4. Mix in broth, bring to simmer, and cook until mixture is moist but not wet, approximately eight minutes. Sprinkle with salt and pepper to taste.
5. Move mixture to container, allow to cool slightly, then cover and place in your fridge until completely cool, approximately 1 hour.
6. Mix in Monterey Jack and cilantro. (Filling can be placed in your fridge for maximum 2 days.)

POBLANO AND CORN FILLING

Ingredients:

- ¾ cup frozen corn, thawed
- 1 teaspoon ground coriander
- 1 teaspoon ground cumin
- 1 teaspoon minced fresh oregano or ¼ teaspoon dried
- 12 ounces (2 to 3) poblano chiles, stemmed, seeded, and chopped fine
- 2 garlic cloves, minced
- 2 tablespoons unsalted butter
- 3 scallions, white parts minced, green parts cut thin
- 4 ounces pepper Jack cheese, shredded (1 cup)
- 4 ounces queso fresco, crumbled (1 cup)
- Salt and pepper

Directions:

1. Melt butter in 12 inch frying pan on moderate heat. Put in poblanos and scallion whites and cook until tender and mildly browned, approximately eight minutes.
2. Mix in garlic, oregano, cumin, coriander, and ¼ teaspoon salt and cook until aromatic, approximately half a minute.
3. Mix in corn and sprinkle with salt and pepper to taste. Move mixture to container, allow to cool slightly, then cover and place in your fridge until completely cool, approximately 1 hour.

4. Mix in pepper Jack, queso fresco, and scallion greens. (Filling can be placed in your fridge for maximum 2 days.)

FRESH MARGARITAS

Yield: approximately four cups; serves four to 6

The best Margaritas are those made at home!

CLASSIC MARGARITAS

It is a good idea to steep for full one day, if possible. If you need to serve margaritas instantly, omit the zest and skip the steeping process altogether.

Ingredients:

- ¼ cup superfine sugar
- 1 cup 100 percent agave tequila, if possible reposado
- 1 cup triple sec
- 2 cups crushed ice
- 4 teaspoons finely grated lemon zest plus ½ cup juice (3 lemons)
- 4 teaspoons finely grated lime zest plus ½ cup juice (4 limes)
- Pinch salt

Directions:

1. Mix lime zest and juice, lemon zest and juice, sugar, and salt in 2 cup liquid measuring cup; cover and place in your fridge until flavors meld, minimum 4 hours or maximum one day.
2. Split 1 cup crushed ice among four to 6 margarita or twofold old fashioned glasses. Strain juice mixture into 1 quart pitcher or cocktail shaker; discard solids. Put in tequila, triple sec, and remaining 1 cup crushed ice; stir or shake until meticulously blended and chilled, 20 to 60 seconds. Strain into ice filled glasses and serve instantly.

STRAWBERRY MARGARITAS

The strawberry flavor in this variation makes the zest and steeping process redundant.

Ingredients:

- ¼ cup superfine sugar
- ½ cup Chambord
- ½ cup lemon juice (3 lemons)
- ½ cup lime juice (4 limes)
- 1 cup 100 percent agave tequila, if possible reposado
- 1 cup triple sec
- 2 cups crushed ice
- 5 ounces strawberries, hulled (1 cup)
- Pinch salt

Directions:

1. Process strawberries, lime juice, lemon juice, sugar, and salt in blender until the desired smoothness is achieved, approximately half a minute.
2. Split 1 cup crushed ice among four to 6 margarita or twofold old fashioned glasses. Strain juice mixture into 1 quart pitcher or cocktail shaker; discard solids. Put in tequila, triple sec, Chambord, and remaining 1 cup crushed ice; stir or shake until meticulously blended and chilled, 20 to 60 seconds. Strain into ice filled glasses and serve instantly.

GROUND MEAT MARINATED IN LIME JUICE (CARNE COCIDA EN LIMÓN)

Yield: Servings 4

A great snack to go with drinks!

Ingredients:

- ½ cup (125 ml) fresh lime juice
- 2 tablespoons finely chopped white onion
- 4 ounces (115 g) tomatoes, finely chopped (⅔ cup/165 ml)
- 4 serrano chiles, finely chopped
- 8 ounces (225 g) freshly ground sirloin, absolutely free of fat
- Salt to taste

Directions:

1. Combine the lime juice well into the ground meat and set it aside to "cook" in your fridge for minimum 4 hours in a nonreactive container.
2. Stir in the remaining ingredients and set the meat aside to season for minimum 2 hours more.
3. Serve with crisp tortillas, either toasted or fried.

HOMEMADE BAKED TORTILLA CHIPS

Yield: 2½ ounces; serves 2 to 3

Tortilla chips for when you're looking to cut your oil intake.

Ingredients:

- 5 (6 inch) corn tortillas
- Kosher salt
- Vegetable oil spray

Directions:

1. Adjust oven rack to middle position and heat oven to 350 degrees. Spray both sides of tortillas liberally with oil spray, then cut each tortilla into 6 wedges. Sprinkle with salt and spread into single layer on baking sheet.
2. Bake tortillas, stirring once in a while, until golden and crunchy, fifteen to twenty minutes. Remove chips from oven and allow to cool before you serve. (Cooled chips can be stored at room temperature for maximum four days.)

HOMEMADE FRIED TORTILLA CHIPS

Yield: 4 ounces; serves 4

These super crisp tortilla chips are exactly how they are meant to be enjoyed.

Ingredients:

- 5 cups peanut oil
- 8 (6 inch) corn tortillas
- Kosher salt

Directions:

1. Cut each tortilla into 6 wedges. Coat 2 baking sheets with several layers of paper towels. Heat oil in Dutch oven over moderate high heat to 350 degrees.
2. Put in half of tortillas and fry until golden and crisp around edges, 2 to 4 minutes. Move fried chips to prepared sheet, drizzle lightly with salt, and allow to cool. Repeat with remaining tortillas and serve. (Cooled chips can be stored at room temperature for maximum four days.)

LITTLE PIECES OF BROWNED PORK (CARNITAS)

Yield: Servings 6

This succulent and delicious recipe is loved all over Mexico!

Ingredients:

- 2 teaspoons salt, or to taste
- 3 pounds (1.35 kg) boneless pork shoulder, with fat

Directions:

1. Chop the meat, with the fat, into strips about 2 by ¾ inches (5 by 2 cm). Barely cover the meat with water in a heavy, wide pan. Put in the salt and bring to its boiling point, uncovered. Reduce the heat and allow the meat to carry on cooking briskly until all the liquid has vaporized—by this time it must be thoroughly cooked but not falling apart.
2. Reduce the heat a little and carry on cooking the meat until all the fat has rendered out of it. Keep turning the meat until it is mildly browned all over—total cooking time is approximately 1 hour and ten minutes.
3. Serve instantly for best flavor and texture.

MEXICAN STYLE SHRIMP COCKTAIL

Yield: Servings 6

A cool, stylish, and mildly spicy appetizer for all the shrimp lovers!

Ingredients:

- ¼ cup chopped fresh cilantro, stems reserved

- ½ cup ketchup
- 1 avocado, halved, pitted, and slice into ½ inch pieces
- 1 cucumber, peeled, halved along the length, seeded, and slice into ½ inch pieces
- 1 small red onion, chopped fine
- 1 tablespoon hot sauce
- 1 tablespoon sugar
- 1 teaspoon black peppercorns
- 1½ pounds medium shrimp (41 to 50 per pound), peeled, deveined, and tails removed
- 2 cups Clamato juice
- 2 tablespoons lime juice, plus lime wedges for serving
- 3 tomatoes, cored and slice into ½ inch pieces
- Salt and pepper

Directions:

1. Mix shrimp, 3 cups water, cilantro stems, peppercorns, sugar, and 1 teaspoon salt in big deep cooking pan. Put deep cooking pan on moderate heat and cook, stirring once in a while, until shrimp are pink and firm to touch, about eight to ten minutes (water must be just bubbling around edge of deep cooking pan and register 165 degrees). Remove deep cooking pan from heat, cover, and let shrimp sit in cooking liquid for a couple of minutes.
2. In the meantime, fill big container with ice water. Drain shrimp into colander, discarding cilantro stems and spices. Instantly move shrimp to ice water to stop cooking and

chill meticulously, approximately 3 minutes. Remove shrimp from ice water and meticulously pat dry using paper towels.

3. Mix tomatoes, cucumber, onion, Clamato juice, ketchup, lime juice, and hot sauce together in serving container. Mix in shrimp, cover, and place in your fridge for minimum 30 minutes. (Shrimp cocktail can be placed in your fridge for maximum one day; allow it to sit at room temperature for about ten minutes before you serve.) Mix in avocado and chopped cilantro and sprinkle with salt and pepper to taste and serve.

MOLLETES

Yield: Servings 6

A popular snack common in Mexican restaurants and coffee shops, as well as many street food stalls.

Ingredients:

- ½ cup finely chopped onion
- ½ cup fresh cilantro leaves
- 1 (16 inch) loaf French or Italian bread
- 1 cup refried beans
- 1 garlic clove, minced
- 1 jalapeño chile, stemmed, seeded, and minced
- 2 tablespoons lime juice

- 3 tomatoes, cored and chopped
- 4 tablespoons unsalted butter, softened
- 8 ounces mild cheddar cheese, shredded (2 cups)
- Salt and pepper

Directions:

1. Toss tomatoes with ¼ teaspoon salt in colander and allow to drain for half an hour As tomatoes drain, layer onion, cilantro, jalapeño, and garlic on top. Shake colander to drain off and discard surplus tomato juice. Move mixture to container, mix in lime juice, and sprinkle with salt and pepper to taste.

2. Adjust oven rack to middle position and heat oven to 400 degrees. Coat baking sheet with aluminum foil. Slice bread in half horizontally, then remove all but ¼ inch of interior crumb; reserve removed crumb for future use. Spread butter uniformly inside hollowed bread and place cut side up on prepared sheet. Bake until mildly toasted and browned, approximately eight minutes.

3. Allow the bread to cool slightly, spread refried beans uniformly inside toasted bread and top with cheese. Bake until cheese is just melted, five to seven minutes. Move bread to cutting board, top with salsa, and slice crosswise into 2 inch pieces. Serve warm.

PEPPERED OYSTERS (OSTIONES PIMENTADOS)

Yield: Servings 6 to 8

I know I know, oysters are best enjoyed raw, but hold your judgments until you try this recipe!

Ingredients:

- ½ teaspoon salt, or to taste
- 1 tablespoon fresh lime juice, more if you wish
- 2 mexican bay leaves
- 2 tablespoons olive oil
- 2 teaspoons whole peppercorns
- 4 dozen oysters, shucked, shells and liquid reserved
- 6 garlic cloves

Directions:

1. Heat the liquid from the oysters to the simmering point, then put in the oysters and poach until the edges start to curl, approximately 2 minutes. Drain the oysters, saving for later the broth.
2. Crush the peppercorns with the salt in a molcajete or mortar. Pound in the garlic and progressively put in the lime juice. Last of all, put in about 3 tablespoons of the reserved oyster broth. Mix thoroughly.

3. Heat the olive oil in a frying pan. Put in the bay leaves and the peppercorn mixture and cook using high heat for approximately 3 minutes. Take away the pan from the heat and put in the oysters. Adjust the seasoning, then put in a squeeze of lime juice and slightly more of the oyster liquid if you wish.
4. Serve warm or at room temperature in half shells.

PICKLED PORK RIND (CHICHARRÓN EN ESCABECHE)

Yield: Servings 6

Ingredients:

- ¼ cup (65 ml) vegetable oil
- ½ teaspoon dried mexican oregano
- ½ teaspoon salt, or to taste
- 1 avocado, peeled and cut
- 1½ cups (375 ml) vinegar, mild or diluted with ½ cup (125 ml) water, roughly
- 2 jalapeño chiles en escabeche, cut into strips
- 2 medium purple onions, thickly cut
- 3 sprigs fresh thyme or ⅛ teaspoon dried
- 6 garlic cloves, left whole
- 8 ounces (225 g) chicharron (Fried pork belly), the thinner the better, broken into two-inch (5-cm) squares

- Freshly ground pepper

Directions:

1. Heat the oil and lightly fry the onions and garlic without browning for approximately 2 minutes. Put in the vinegar, oregano, thyme, salt, and pepper to the pan and bring to its boiling point. Put in the chicharrón pieces and chiles and cook over quite high heat while stirring occasionally to prevent sticking, until the chicharrón has tenderized and absorbed almost all the vinegar—about five minutes. Set aside to cool, then serve, topped with slices of avocado.
2. To my mind, chicharrón en escabeche is best served the moment it has cooled off, but it will keep indefinitely in your fridge (although it congeals and must be brought up to room temperature before you serve).

PUMPKIN SEED DIP (SIKIL P'AK)

Yield: about 3 cups

A classic hummus-like dip that is enjoyed in the Yucatán peninsula.

Ingredients:

- ¼ cup extra virgin olive oil
- 1 habanero chile, stemmed, seeded, and chopped
- 1 onion, chopped

- 1 pound tomatoes, cored and halved
- 1½ cups roasted, unhulled pumpkin seeds
- 2 ounces queso fresco, crumbled (½ cup)
- 2 tablespoons chopped fresh cilantro
- 2 tablespoons lime juice
- Salt and pepper

Directions:

1. Adjust 1 oven rack to middle position and second rack 6 inches from broiler element. Heat oven to 400 degrees. Wash pumpkin seeds under warm water and dry meticulously. Spread seeds on rimmed baking sheet, place sheet on lower rack, and toast seeds until a golden-brown colour is achieved, stirring once in a while, twelve to fifteen minutes. Set aside to cool down a little and heat broiler.

2. Coat second rimmed baking sheet with aluminum foil. Toss tomatoes with 1 tablespoon oil and position cut side down on prepared sheet. Put sheet on upper rack and broil until tomatoes are spotty brown, 7 to ten minutes. Move tomatoes to blender and let cool to room temperature.

3. Put in onion, lime juice, habanero, pumpkin seeds, and remaining 3 tablespoon oil to blender and pulse until smooth, approximately 1 minute, scraping down sides of blender as required. Move dip to serving container and place in your fridge until completely chilled, minimum 2 hours or maximum one day. Sprinkle with salt and pepper

to taste. Drizzle with queso fresco and cilantro before you serve.

QUESO FUNDIDO

Yield: Servings 6 to 8

An insanely delicious table dip of Mexican table cheese served with toppings.

Ingredients:

- ½ small onion, cut thin
- 1 poblano chile, stemmed, seeded, and cut thin
- 1 teaspoon vegetable oil
- 4 ounces Mexican style chorizo sausage, casings removed
- 6 (8 inch) corn or flour tortillas, warmed and slice into wedges
- 8 ounces queso de Oaxaca, cut into ½ inch pieces

Directions:

1. Adjust oven rack to lower middle position and heat oven to 375 degrees. Heat oil in 12 inch nonstick frying pan over moderate high heat until shimmering. Put in chorizo and cook, breaking up meat with wooden spoon, until fat starts to render, approximately one minute. Mix in poblano and onion and cook until chorizo and vegetables are

thoroughly browned, five to seven minutes. Drain chorizo mixture in colander.

2. Spread queso Oaxaca uniformly into 9 inch pie plate, then drizzle with drained chorizo mixture. Move pie plate to oven and bake until cheese is just melted, about eight to ten minutes. Serve instantly with tortillas.

RICH WELL-FRIED BEANS FROM JALISCO (FRIJOLES PUERCOS ESTILO JALISCO)

Yield: Servings 6

My personal favourite variation of the classic frijoles puercos.

Ingredients:

- 1 chorizo, approximately 3 ounces (85 g)
- 2 jalapeño chiles en escabeche
- 2 tablespoons finely grated queso ranchero or romano
- 20 small, pitted green olives, chopped
- 6 strips bacon
- 8 ounces (225 g) pinto or pink beans, cooked—3½ to 4 cups (875 ml to 1 l) with broth
- Lard as required
- toasted tortillas or totopos

Directions:

1. Skin and crumble the chorizo, and cut the bacon. Cook in a frying pan using low heat, covered, until most of the fat has rendered out. Be careful not to allow them to burn. Remove chorizo and bacon and save for later.
2. There must be about ⅓ cup (85 ml) fat in the pan. Take out or make up to that amount with lard. Put in the beans and broth and cook them using high heat, mashing them. If they start to dry out and cling to the pan, put in slightly more lard.
3. Once the beans are mashed to a coarse texture and are almost dry, ready to roll, put in the bacon and about two thirds of the olives, chiles, and chorizo.
4. Roll the beans, then turn onto the serving dish and top with the rest of the olives, chiles, and chorizo.
5. Drizzle the roll with the cheese and serve with the toasted tortillas or totopos.

ROE SNACK (CAVIAR DE CHAPALA CARP)

Yield: Servings 6

A delicious Mexican appetizer usually served with hot tortillas other small sides to nibble on.

Ingredients:

- ¼ cup (65 ml) vegetable or olive oil
- 1 garlic clove, finely chopped
- 1 pound (450 g) carp roe

- 1 tablespoon salt
- 2 tablespoons finely chopped white onion
- About 6 ounces (180 g) tomatoes, finely chopped (approximately 1 cup/250 ml)

The toppings

- ⅓ cup (85 ml) finely chopped cilantro
- ⅓ cup (85 ml) finely chopped green, unripe tomatoes or tomate verde
- ⅓ cup (85 ml) finely chopped serrano chiles or any other fresh, hot green chiles
- ½ cup (125 ml) finely chopped white onion

Directions:

1. Place the salt and enough water to cover the roe in a shallow pan and bring to the simmering point. Put in the roe and allow it to simmer for eight to ten minutes, depending on thickness, then remove and drain. When it is sufficiently cool to handle, take off the skin and crumble the roe.
2. Heat the oil in a heavy pan. Put in the tomatoes, onion, and garlic and fry over quite high heat while stirring occasionally and scraping the bottom of the pan, until the onion is tender and the mixture is almost dry. Put in the crumbled roe with salt to taste and carry on frying the mixture on moderate heat, flipping it over continuously, until dry and crumbly, approximately five minutes.

3. Serve hot, accompanied by the onion and the other finely chopped toppings, in small different bowls, and a pile of hot corn tortillas.

SEAFOOD COCKTAIL (MARISCOS A LA MARINERA)

Yield: Servings 6

Any seafood ingredient of your choice will do the job here: raw clams or scallops, abalone, conch, or cooked shrimps.

Ingredients:

- ½ cup (125 ml) fresh lime juice
- 1 big avocado, cubed
- 1 small white onion, finely chopped (about ¼ cup/65 ml)
- 2 heaped tablespoons finely chopped cilantro
- 3 dozen big raw clams or scallops or medium-size cooked shrimps
- 3 tablespoons olive oil
- 3 to 4 serrano chiles or any fresh, hot green chiles, finely chopped with seeds
- About 12 ounces (340 g) tomatoes, finely chopped (about 2 cups/500 ml)
- Salt and freshly ground pepper to taste

Directions:

1. If you are using clams, open them or have them opened for you, saving both the clams and their juice. If you are using scallops, allow them to marinate in the lime juice for about 1 hour or so.
2. Mix the clams (and their liquid) or other seafood with the remaining ingredients, tweak the seasoning, and serve slightly chilled.

SHREDDED CRABMEAT AND VEGETABLES (SALPICÓN DE JAIBA)

Yield: enough to fill 12 small tortillas

This salpicón makes a scrumptious filling for small tacos and can also be served with plain white rice.

Ingredients:

- ¼ cup (65 ml) vegetable oil
- ⅓ cup (85 ml) finely chopped white onion
- ½ cup (125 ml) finely chopped celery
- 1 cup (250 ml) cooked, shredded crabmeat
- 3 tablespoons finely chopped cilantro
- 5 serrano chiles, finely chopped, with seeds
- Salt to taste

Directions:

1. Heat the oil in a frying pan and cook the onion gently until translucent.
2. Put in the celery, chiles, and crabmeat and fry until they barely start to brown mildly. The mixture must be rather dry. Finally, put in the cilantro and salt and cook for a minute more.
3. Serve with hot tortillas.

SHRIMP AND LIME CEVICHE

Yield: Servings 6

Usually served with crispy tortilla chips or used as a topping for tostadas, this simple and delicious seafood appetizer is quite uplifting.

Ingredients:

- ¼ cup extra virgin olive oil
- ½ cup lemon juice (3 lemons)
- ½ teaspoon sugar
- 1 garlic clove, minced
- 1 jalapeño chile, stemmed, seeded, and minced
- 1 pound extra big shrimp (21 to 25 per pound), peeled, deveined, tails removed, and halved along the length
- 1 teaspoon grated lime zest plus ½ cup juice (4 limes)
- 1 tomato, cored, seeded, and chopped fine
- 3 tablespoons minced fresh cilantro

- 4 scallions, cut thin
- Salt and pepper

Directions:

1. Mix tomato, lemon juice, jalapeño, lime zest and juice, garlic, and ½ teaspoon salt in medium container. Mix in shrimp, cover, and place in your fridge until shrimp are firm and opaque throughout, forty-five minutes to an hour, stirring midway through refrigerating.
2. Drain shrimp mixture in colander, leaving shrimp slightly wet, and move to serving container. Mix in oil, scallions, cilantro, and sugar. Sprinkle with salt and pepper to taste and serve.

SINALOAN SHREDDED BEEF (MOCHOMOS SINALOENSES)

Yield: about 6 cups (1.5 l)

An insanely popular dish from Sinaloa, made of carne machaca, or machacada.

Ingredients:

- ½ cup (125 ml) lard or vegetable oil
- 1 poblano chile, charred, peeled, cleaned, and cut into little squares
- 1½ tablespoons coarse sea salt

- 2 pounds (900 g) round steak (with some fat on)
- 8 ounces (225 g) white onions, roughly cut

Directions:

1. Chop the meat into 1-inch (2.5-cm) cubes. Put the meat in a single layer in a big pan. Put in the salt and water to barely cover. Bring the water to its boiling point, reduce the heat, and cook slowly, uncovered, until the water has vaporized and the meat is soft but not too soft—thirty-five to forty minutes. Continue drying the meat out using low heat so that it is dried and slightly crusty on the outside. Let cool.
2. Put 3 pieces of the meat into a blender and blend at moderate speed until meat is finely shredded. Continue in similarly until all the meat has been shredded.
3. Heat half of the lard in a frying pan, put in the onions, and fry for a short period of time for approximately 1 minute—they must be crisp and still opaque. Take away the onions using a slotted spoon and drain. Set aside.
4. Put in the rest of the lard to the frying pan, heat, put in the shredded meat and chile, and stir until the meat is well thoroughly heated and just browning—5 to 8 minutes.
5. Mix in the onions, heat through, and serve instantly.

STUFFED JALAPEÑOS

Yield: Servings 6 to 8

The only thing better than jalapeños are stuffed jalapeños.

Ingredients:

- 1 big egg yolk
- 1 teaspoon ground cumin
- 12 jalapeño chiles, halved along the length with stems left undamaged, seeds and ribs removed
- 2 scallions, cut thin
- 2 tablespoons panko bread crumbs
- 2 teaspoons lime juice
- 3 tablespoons minced fresh cilantro
- 4 ounces cream cheese, softened
- 4 ounces mild cheddar cheese, shredded (1 cup)
- 4 ounces Monterey Jack cheese, shredded (1 cup)
- 6 slices bacon
- Salt

Directions:

1. Adjust oven rack to upper middle position and heat oven to 500 degrees. Set wire rack in rimmed baking sheet. Cook bacon in 12 inch nonstick frying pan on moderate heat until crunchy, 7 to 9 minutes. Using slotted spoon, move bacon to paper towel–lined plate. When bacon is sufficiently cool to handle, cut fine and save for later.
2. Season jalapeños with salt and place cut side down on prepared rack. Bake until just starting to tenderize, approximately five minutes. Remove jalapeños from oven

and reduce oven temperature to 450 degrees. When sufficiently cool to handle, flip jalapeños cut side up.

3. Mix cheddar, Monterey Jack, cream cheese, scallions, cilantro, panko, egg yolk, lime juice, cumin, and bacon together in container until meticulously blended. Split cheese mixture among jalapeños, pushing into cavities. (Filled jalapeños can be covered and placed in the fridge for maximum one day.)
4. Bake jalapeños until soft and filling is mildly browned, 9 to 14 minutes. Allow to cool for five minutes and serve.

TOMATILLO AND PINTO BEAN NACHOS

Yield: Servings four to 6

Try this recipe when you're in mood for a crunchy vegetarian snack!

Ingredients:

- ½ cup sour cream
- 1 (fifteen ounce) can pinto beans, washed
- 1 cup Fresh Tomato Salsa
- 1 cup frozen corn, thawed
- 1 onion, chopped fine
- 1 tablespoon vegetable oil
- 1 teaspoon ground coriander
- 1 teaspoon salt

- 1½ cups Chunky Guacamole
- 12 ounces pepper Jack cheese, shredded (3 cups)
- 12 ounces tomatillos, husks and stems removed, washed well, dried, and slice into ½ inch pieces
- 2 jalapeño chiles, stemmed and cut thin
- 2 teaspoons minced fresh oregano or ½ teaspoon dried
- 3 garlic cloves, minced
- 3 radishes, trimmed and cut thin
- 8 ounces tortilla chips
- Lime wedges

Directions:

1. Adjust oven rack to middle position and heat oven to 400 degrees. Heat oil in 12 inch nonstick frying pan on moderate heat until shimmering. Put in onion and cook until tender, approximately five minutes. Mix in garlic, coriander, salt, and oregano and cook until aromatic, approximately half a minute. Put in tomatillos and corn, decrease the heat to moderate low, and cook until tomatillos have released all their moisture and mixture is nearly dry, approximately ten minutes. Allow to cool slightly.

2. Spread half of tortilla chips uniformly into 13 by 9 inch baking dish. Drizzle 1½ cups pepper Jack uniformly over chips, then top uniformly with half of tomatillo mixture, followed by half of beans and, finally, half of jalapeños. Repeat layering with remaining chips, pepper Jack,

tomatillo mixture, beans, and jalapeños. Bake until cheese is melted and just starting to brown, 7 to ten minutes.

3. Let nachos cool for a couple of minutes, then drizzle with radishes. Drop scoops of guacamole, salsa, and sour cream around edges of nachos. Serve instantly, passing lime wedges separately.

BEEF NACHOS

Yield: Servings four to 6

The name pretty much says it all!

Ingredients:

- ⅛ teaspoon salt
- ¼ teaspoon cayenne pepper
- ½ cup sour cream
- ½ teaspoon ground coriander
- ½ teaspoon ground cumin
- 1 cup Fresh Tomato Salsa
- 1 garlic clove, minced
- 1 pound cheddar cheese, shredded (4 cups)
- 1 small onion, chopped fine
- 1 tablespoon chili powder
- 1 teaspoon minced fresh oregano or ¼ teaspoon dried
- 1½ cups Chunky Guacamole
- 2 big jalapeño chiles, stemmed and cut thin

- 2 scallions, cut thin
- 2 teaspoons vegetable oil
- 8 ounces 90 percent lean ground beef
- 8 ounces tortilla chips
- Lime wedges

Directions:

1. Adjust oven rack to middle position and heat oven to 400 degrees. Heat oil in 12 inch frying pan on moderate heat until shimmering. Put in onion and cook until tender, approximately 3 minutes. Mix in chili powder, garlic, oregano, cumin, coriander, cayenne, and salt and cook until aromatic, approximately half a minute. Put in ground beef and cook, breaking up meat with wooden spoon, until beef is no longer pink, approximately five minutes.
2. Spread half of tortilla chips uniformly into 13 by 9 inch baking dish. Drizzle 2 cups cheddar uniformly over chips, then top uniformly with half of beef mixture, followed by half of jalapeño slices. Repeat layering with remaining chips, cheddar, beef mixture, and jalapeños. Bake until cheese is melted and just starting to brown, 7 to ten minutes.
3. Let nachos cool for a couple of minutes, then drizzle with scallions. Drop scoops of guacamole, salsa, and sour cream around edges of nachos. Serve instantly, passing lime wedges separately.

YUCATECAN PICKLED LIMA BEANS (IBIS ESCABECHADOS)

Yield: about 3 cups (750 ml)

Ibis, both fresh and dried, are common ingredients in the food of the yucatán peninsula. They are quite similar to lima beans.

Ingredients:

- ¼ cup (65 ml) bitter orange juice or fresh lime juice
- ⅓ cup (85 ml) tightly packed, finely chopped cilantro
- ½ habanero chile, finely chopped
- 1 cup (250 ml) loosely packed, thinly cut white onion
- 12 ounces (340 g) ibis or lima beans (about 2½ cups/625 ml)
- Boiling water to cover
- Salt to taste

Directions:

1. Cover the onion with the boiling water and leave to soak for a minute. Drain, put in salt to taste, and mix in the bitter orange juice and chile. Set aside in a nonreactive container at room temperature to macerate while you cook the beans.
2. Put enough water into a small deep cooking pan to cover the beans. Bring the water to its boiling point, put in the beans, and cook on moderate heat until just soft—about

ten minutes. Drain, and while still warm put in to the onion. Mix in the cilantro and put in salt as required. Serve at room temperature.

YUCATECAN PICKLED POTATOES (PAPAS ESCABECHADAS)

Yield: about 2⅔ cups (665 ml)

A popular snack serve in Mexican bars, usually free of charge.

Ingredients:

- ¼ cup (65 ml) bitter orange juice or fresh lime juice
- ⅓ cup (85 ml) tightly packed, finely chopped cilantro
- ½ habanero chile, finely chopped
- 1 cup (250 ml) loosely packed, thinly cut white onion
- 12 ounces (340 g) waxy potatoes, cut into ¾-inch (2-cm) cubes
- Boiling water to cover
- Salt to taste

Directions:

1. Cover the onion with the boiling water and leave to soak for a minute. Drain, put in salt to taste, and mix in the bitter orange juice and chile. Set aside in a nonreactive container at room temperature to macerate while you cook the potatoes.

2. Put enough water into a small deep cooking pan to cover the potatoes. Bring the water to its boiling point, put in the potatoes, and cook on moderate heat until just soft— approximately eight minutes. Drain, cool off a little, and peel—but while still slightly warm put in to the onion. Mix in the cilantro and put in more salt as required. Serve at room temperature.

YUCATECAN SHREDDED MEAT (SALPICÓN YUCATECO OR DZIK DE VENADO)

Yield: Servings 6

Any meat can be used in this recipe. This recipe is a great way to use any leftover meat you might have from a previous meal.

Ingredients:

- ½ cup (125 ml) seville orange juice
- ⅔ cup (165 ml) radishes cut into fine strips
- 1 cup (250 ml) cooked and shredded meat
- 3 tablespoons very finely chopped cilantro
- Salt to taste

Directions:

1. Mix all the ingredients and allow them to season for approximately 30 minutes before you serve.

ABOUT THE AUTHOR

Marissa Marie is a cook, a nutritionist, and a restaurant owner. She was raised in a small city called Los Alamos in New Mexico. Her parents loved to cook, and as a result she too fell in love with the art. Although she learnt a lot from her mother, most of her knowledge comes from self-teaching and experimentation.

Made in the USA
Coppell, TX
22 June 2023

18405885R00066